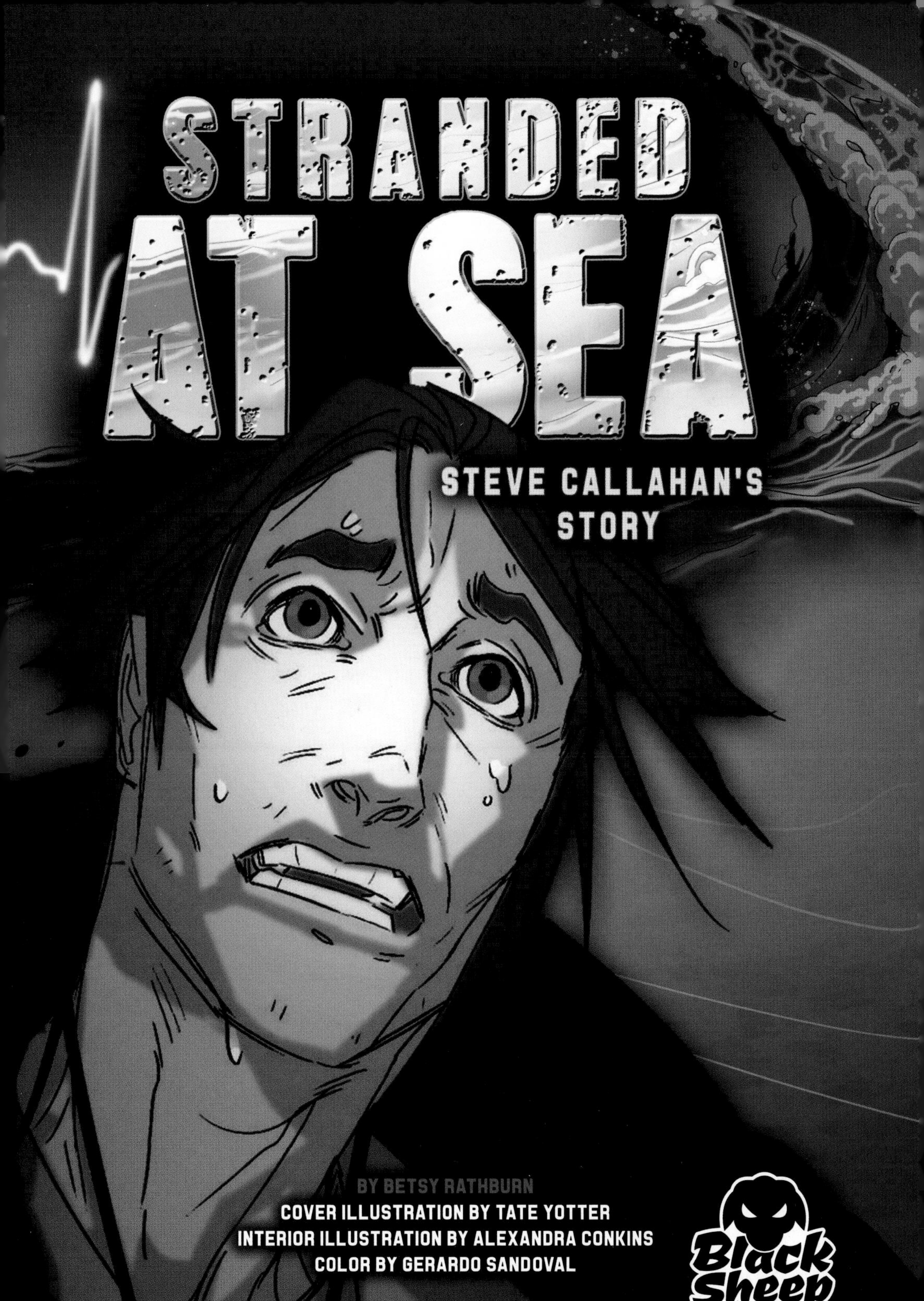

STRANDED AT SEA

STEVE CALLAHAN'S STORY

BY BETSY RATHBURN
COVER ILLUSTRATION BY TATE YOTTER
INTERIOR ILLUSTRATION BY ALEXANDRA CONKINS
COLOR BY GERARDO SANDOVAL

Black Sheep

BELLWETHER MEDIA • MINNEAPOLIS, MN

STRAY FROM REGULAR READS
WITH BLACK SHEEP BOOKS.
FEEL A RUSH WITH EVERY READ!

This edition first published in 2022 by Bellwether Media, Inc.

No part of this publication may be reproduced in whole or in part without written permission of the publisher. For information regarding permission, write to Bellwether Media, Inc., Attention: Permissions Department, 6012 Blue Circle Drive, Minnetonka, MN 55343.

Library of Congress Cataloging-in-Publication Data

LC record for Stranded at Sea: Steve Callahan's Story available at https://lccn.loc.gov/2021025026

Text copyright © 2022 by Bellwether Media, Inc. BLACK SHEEP and associated logos are trademarks and/or registered trademarks of Bellwether Media, Inc.

Editor: Christina Leaf   Designer: Andrea Schneider

Printed in the United States of America, North Mankato, MN.

TABLE OF CONTENTS

Red text identifies historical quotes.

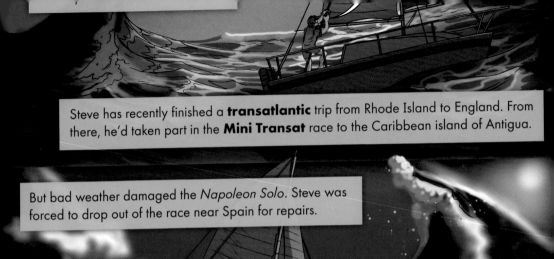

Steve has recently finished a **transatlantic** trip from Rhode Island to England. From there, he'd taken part in the **Mini Transat** race to the Caribbean island of Antigua.

But bad weather damaged the *Napoleon Solo*. Steve was forced to drop out of the race near Spain for repairs.

After four weeks of repairs and a long journey to the Canary Islands, Steve is finally setting off across the Atlantic Ocean. He hopes to make it to the Caribbean before February 25.

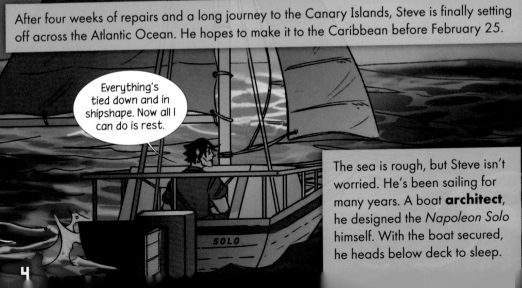

Everything's tied down and in shipshape. Now all I can do is rest.

SOLO

The sea is rough, but Steve isn't worried. He's been sailing for many years. A boat **architect**, he designed the *Napoleon Solo* himself. With the boat secured, he heads below deck to sleep.

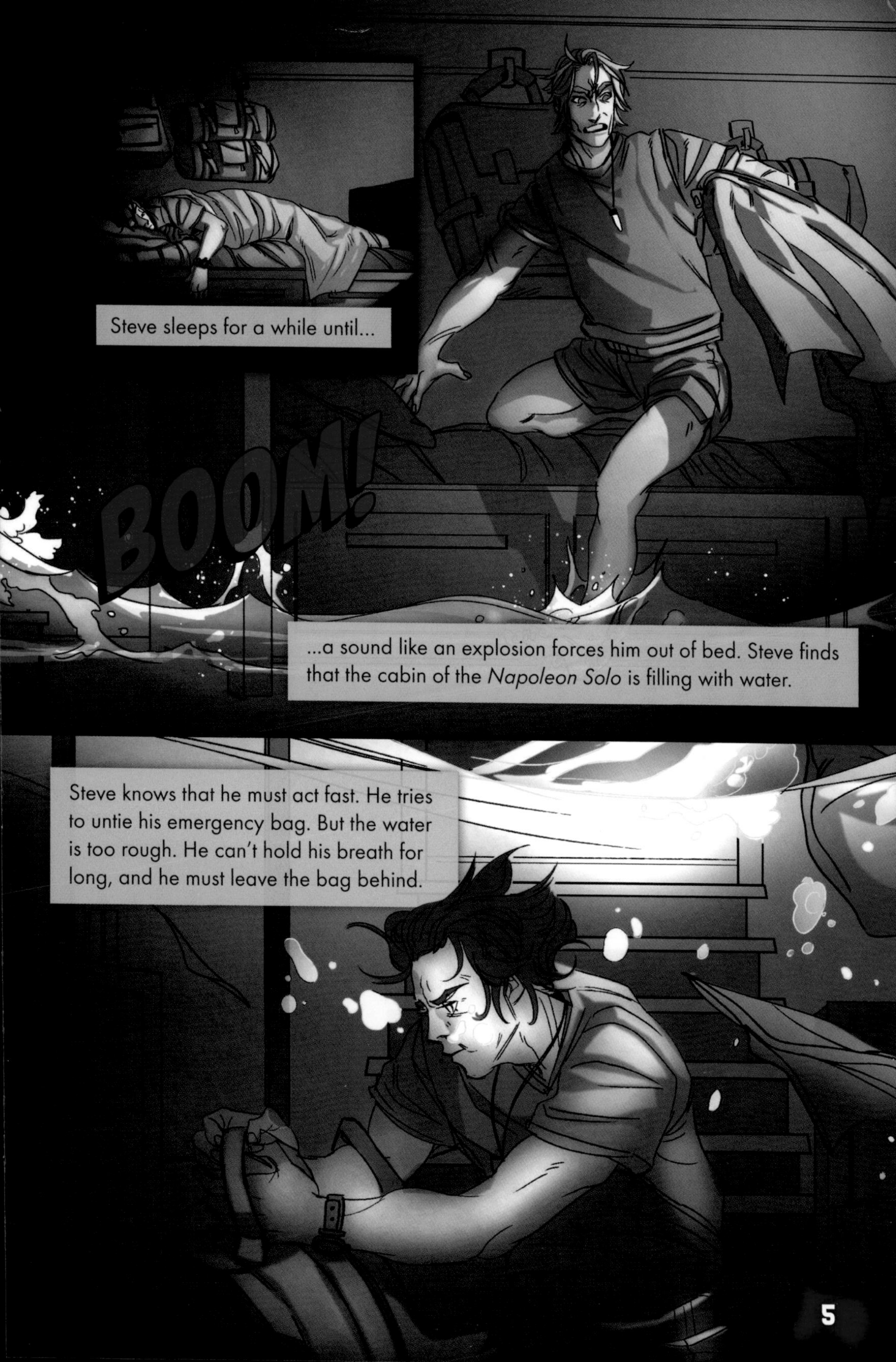
Steve sleeps for a while until...
BOOM!
...a sound like an explosion forces him out of bed. Steve finds that the cabin of the *Napoleon Solo* is filling with water.
Steve knows that he must act fast. He tries to untie his emergency bag. But the water is too rough. He can't hold his breath for long, and he must leave the bag behind.

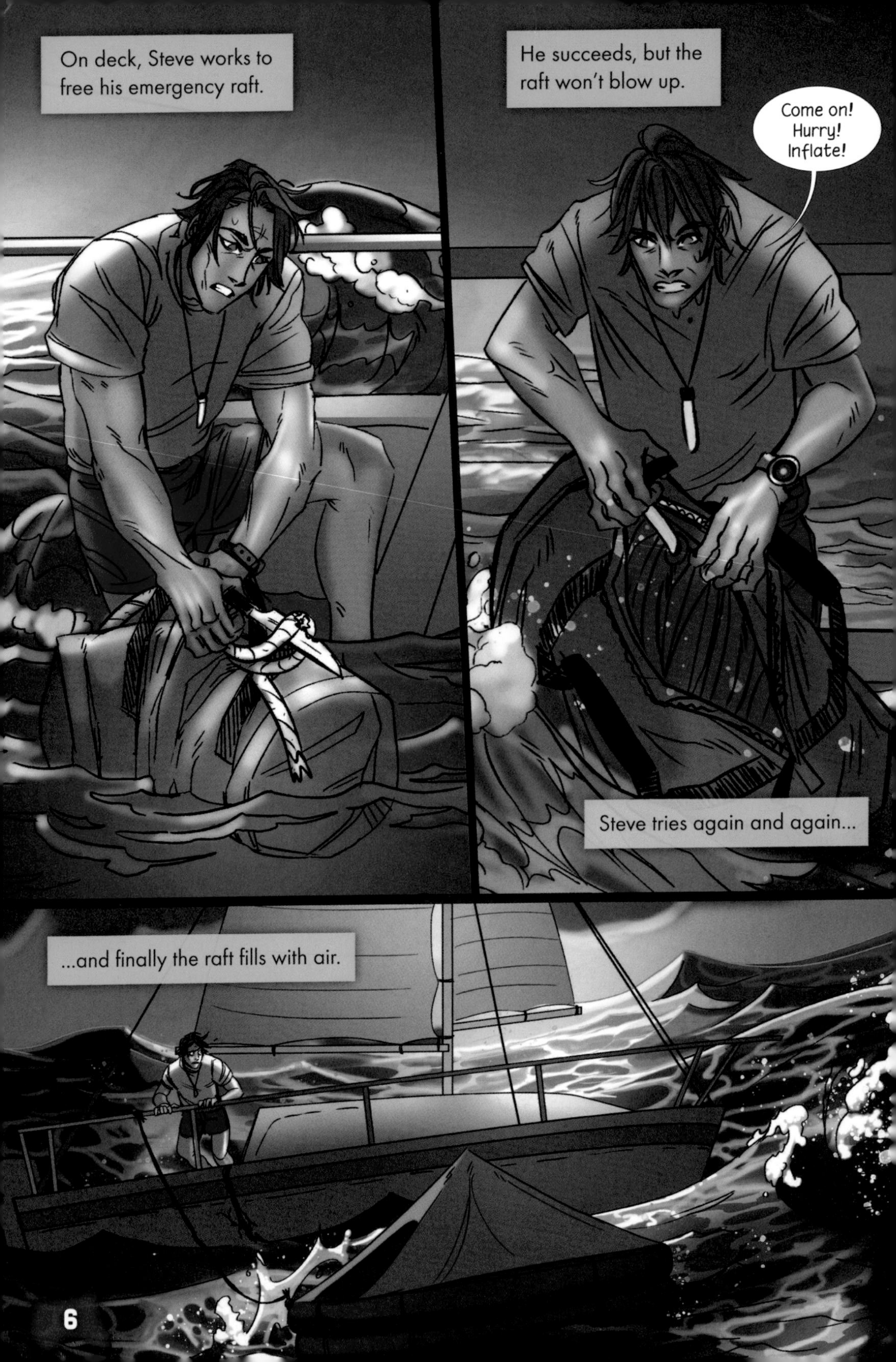
On deck, Steve works to free his emergency raft.
He succeeds, but the raft won't blow up.
Come on! Hurry! Inflate!
Steve tries again and again...
...and finally the raft fills with air.

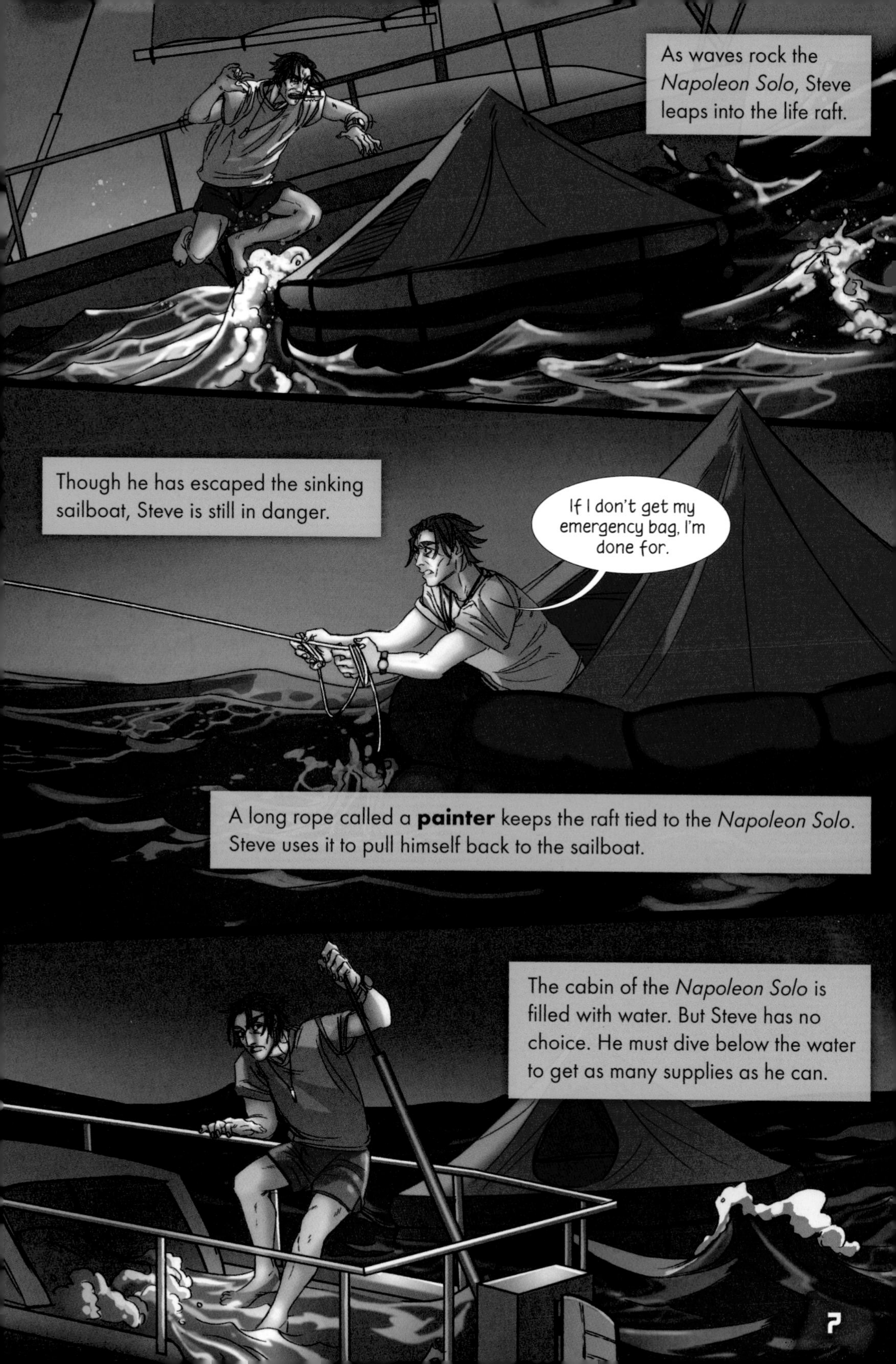

As waves rock the *Napoleon Solo*, Steve leaps into the life raft.
Though he has escaped the sinking sailboat, Steve is still in danger.
If I don't get my emergency bag, I'm done for.
A long rope called a **painter** keeps the raft tied to the *Napoleon Solo*. Steve uses it to pull himself back to the sailboat.
The cabin of the *Napoleon Solo* is filled with water. But Steve has no choice. He must dive below the water to get as many supplies as he can.

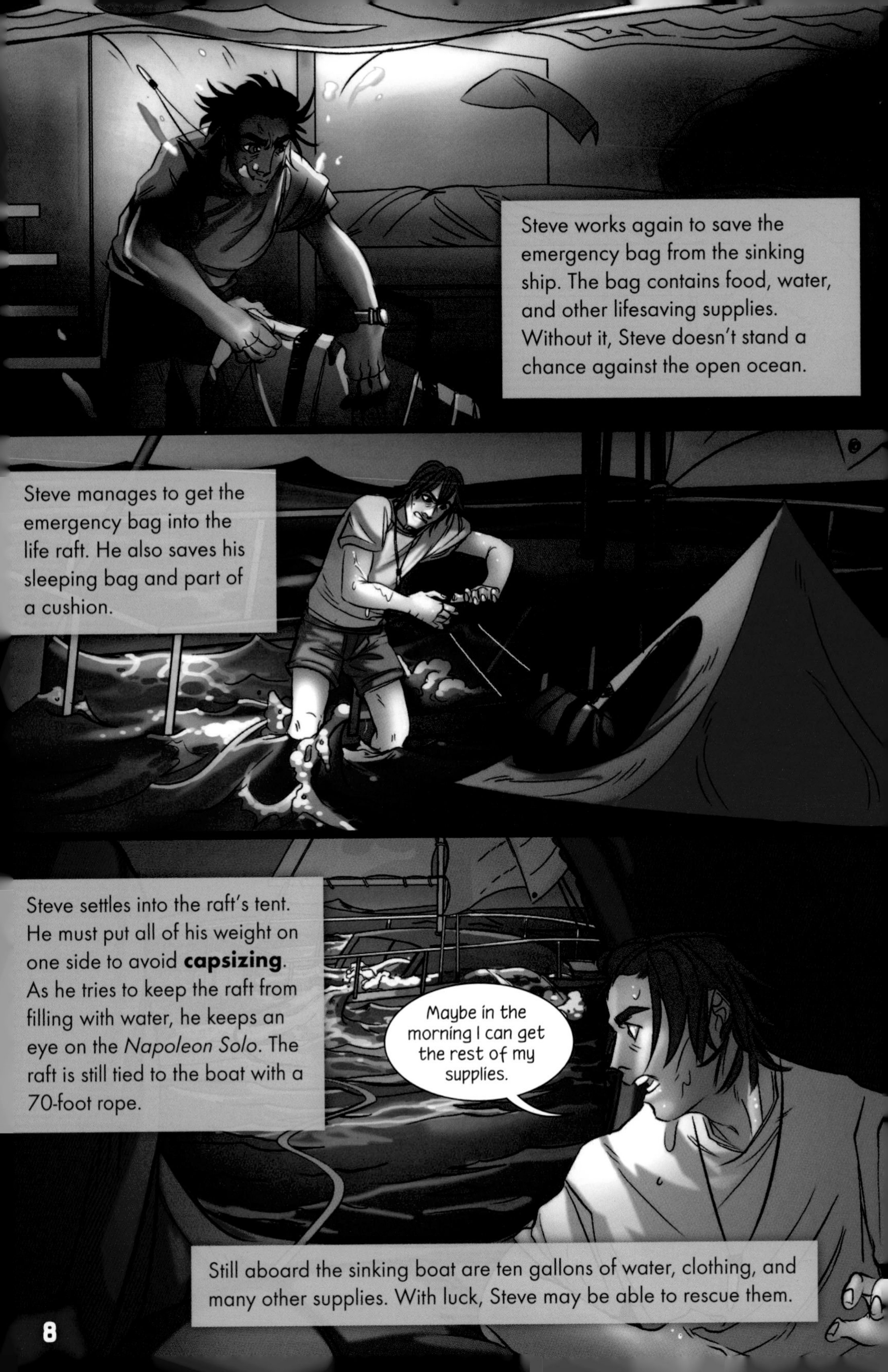
Steve works again to save the emergency bag from the sinking ship. The bag contains food, water, and other lifesaving supplies. Without it, Steve doesn't stand a chance against the open ocean.
Steve manages to get the emergency bag into the life raft. He also saves his sleeping bag and part of a cushion.
Steve settles into the raft's tent. He must put all of his weight on one side to avoid **capsizing**. As he tries to keep the raft from filling with water, he keeps an eye on the *Napoleon Solo*. The raft is still tied to the boat with a 70-foot rope.
Maybe in the morning I can get the rest of my supplies.
Still aboard the sinking boat are ten gallons of water, clothing, and many other supplies. With luck, Steve may be able to rescue them.

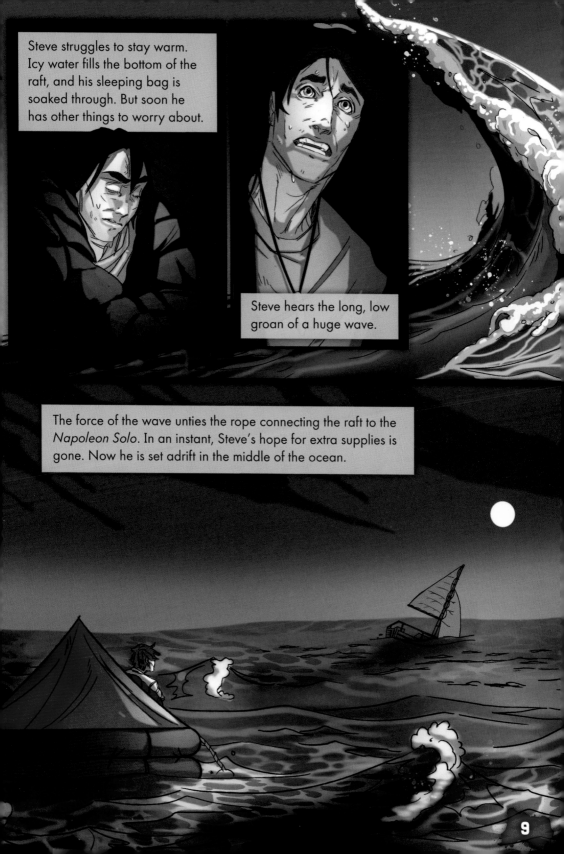

Steve struggles to stay warm. Icy water fills the bottom of the raft, and his sleeping bag is soaked through. But soon he has other things to worry about.

Steve hears the long, low groan of a huge wave.

The force of the wave unties the rope connecting the raft to the *Napoleon Solo*. In an instant, Steve's hope for extra supplies is gone. Now he is set adrift in the middle of the ocean.

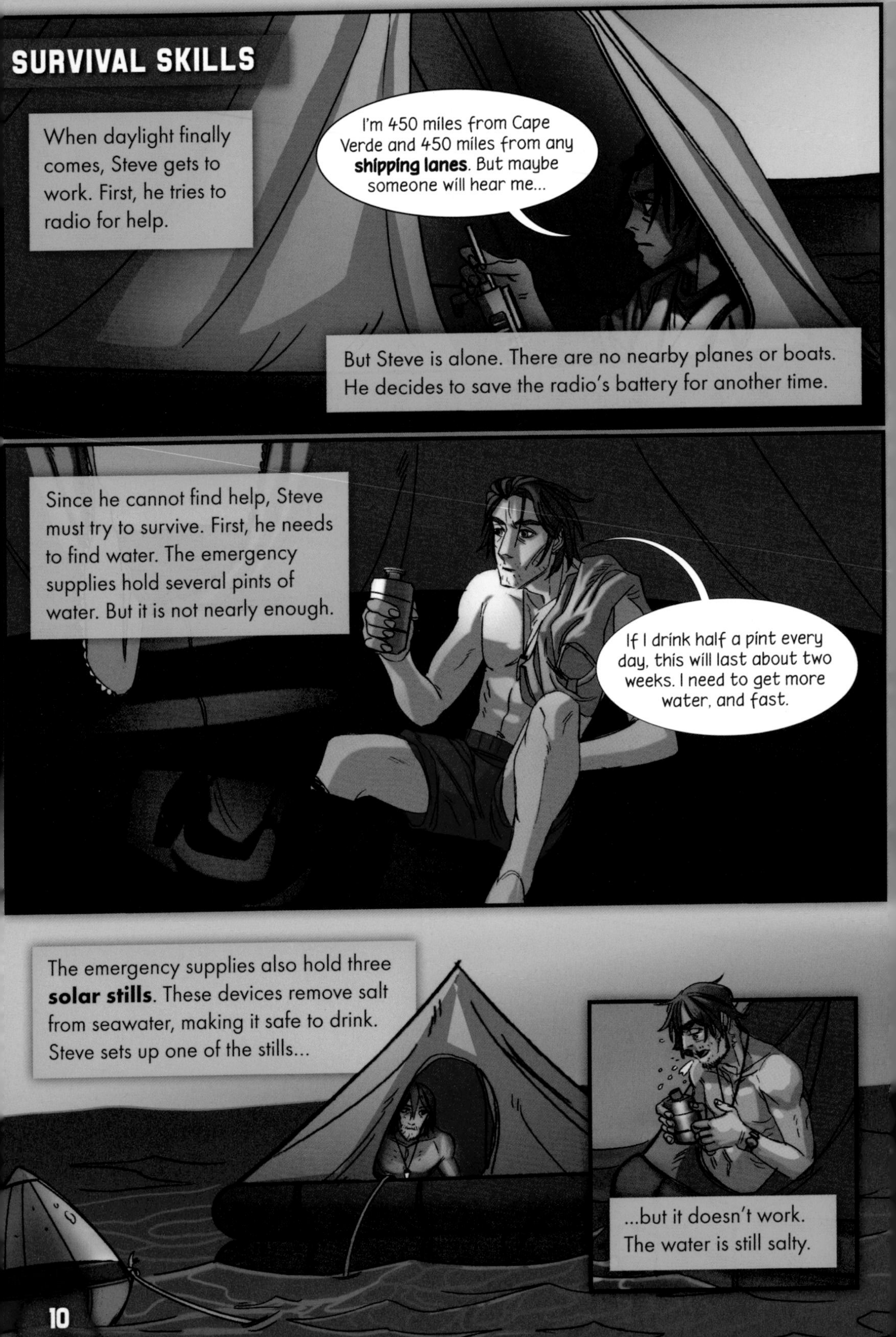
SURVIVAL SKILLS
When daylight finally comes, Steve gets to work. First, he tries to radio for help.
I'm 450 miles from Cape Verde and 450 miles from any **shipping lanes**. But maybe someone will hear me...
But Steve is alone. There are no nearby planes or boats. He decides to save the radio's battery for another time.
Since he cannot find help, Steve must try to survive. First, he needs to find water. The emergency supplies hold several pints of water. But it is not nearly enough.
If I drink half a pint every day, this will last about two weeks. I need to get more water, and fast.
The emergency supplies also hold three **solar stills**. These devices remove salt from seawater, making it safe to drink. Steve sets up one of the stills...
...but it doesn't work. The water is still salty.

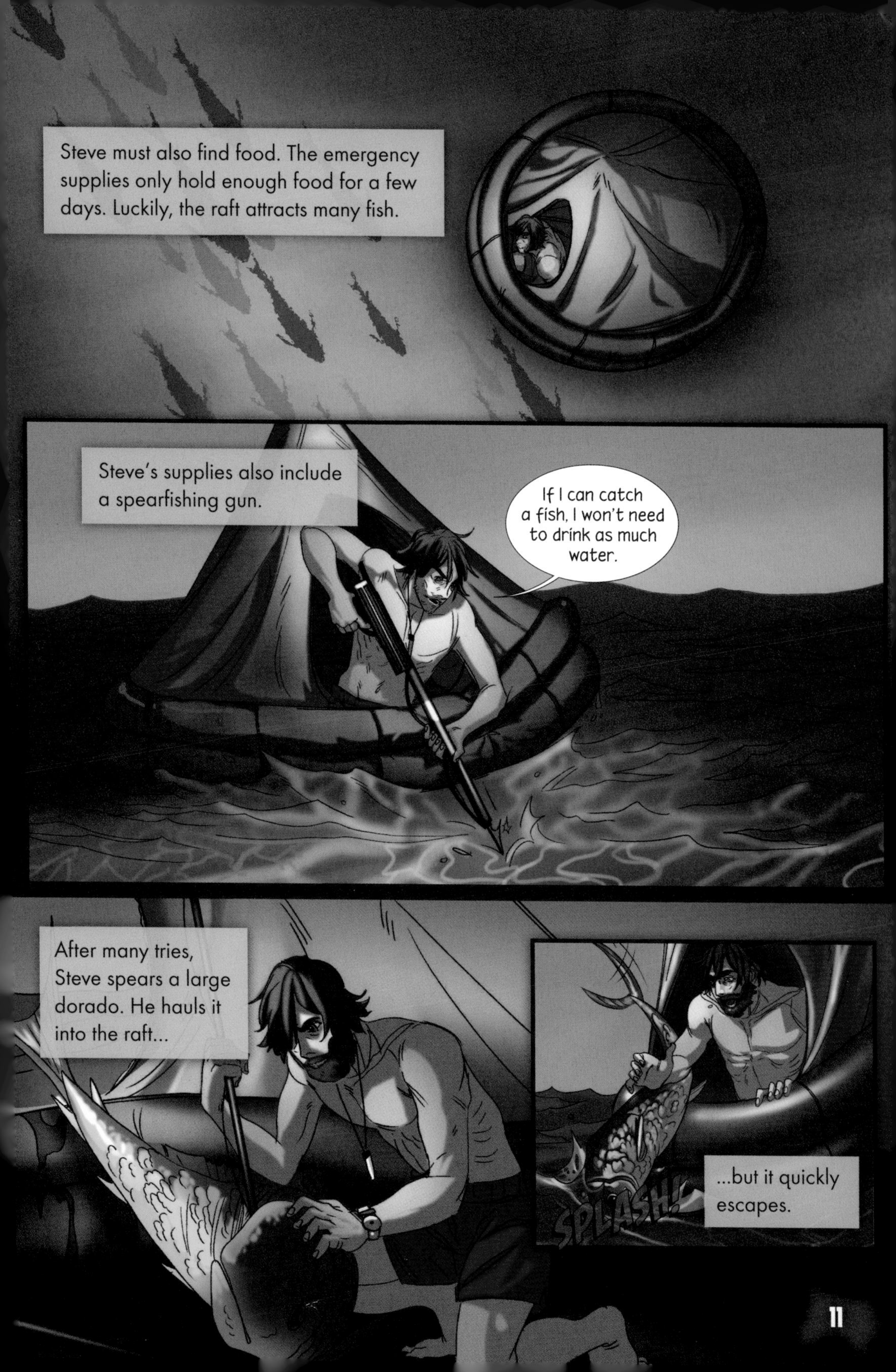
Steve must also find food. The emergency supplies only hold enough food for a few days. Luckily, the raft attracts many fish.
Steve's supplies also include a spearfishing gun.
If I can catch a fish, I won't need to drink as much water.
After many tries, Steve spears a large dorado. He hauls it into the raft...
SPLASH!
...but it quickly escapes.

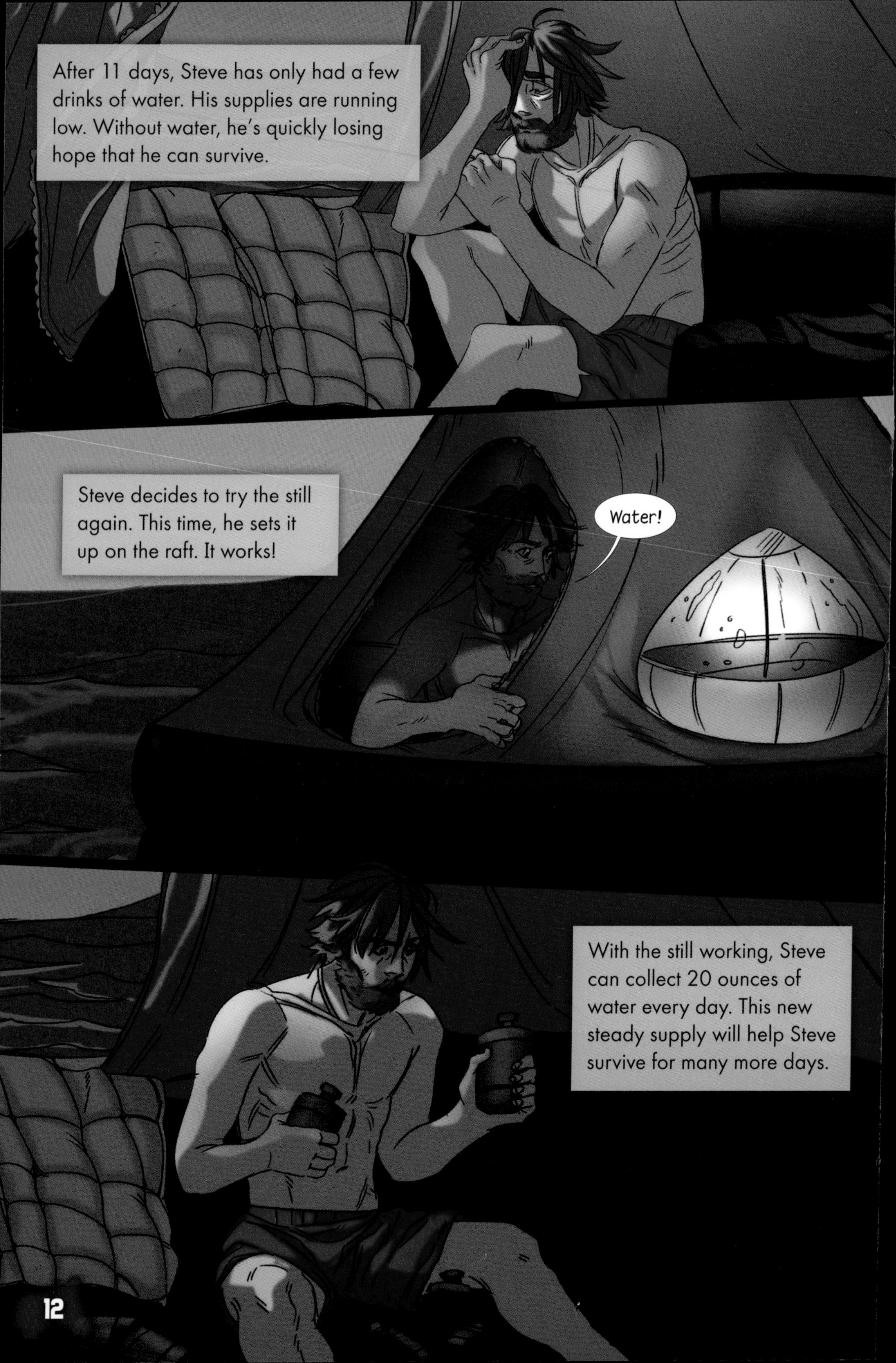
After 11 days, Steve has only had a few drinks of water. His supplies are running low. Without water, he's quickly losing hope that he can survive.
Steve decides to try the still again. This time, he sets it up on the raft. It works!
Water!
With the still working, Steve can collect 20 ounces of water every day. This new steady supply will help Steve survive for many more days.

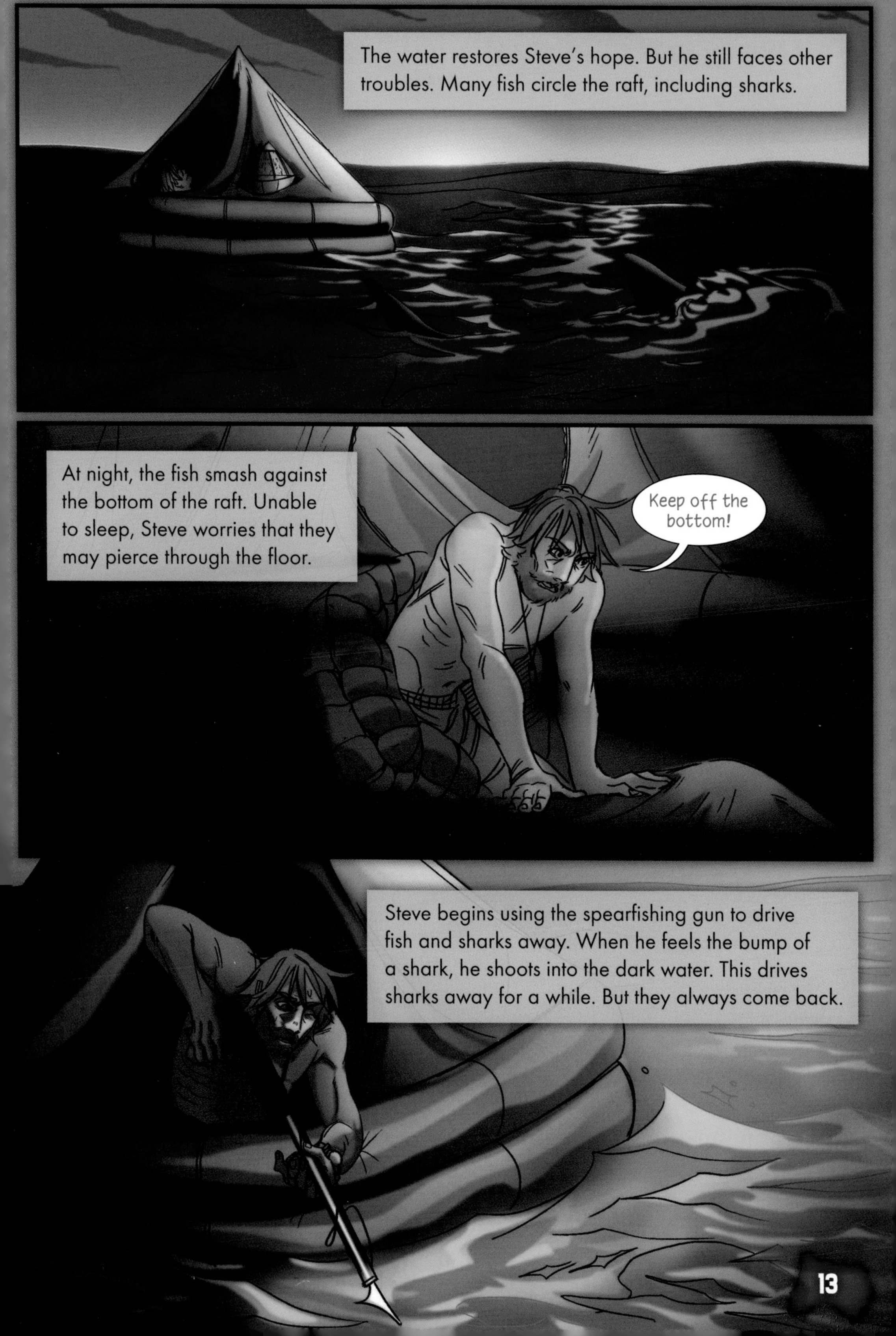
The water restores Steve's hope. But he still faces other troubles. Many fish circle the raft, including sharks.
At night, the fish smash against the bottom of the raft. Unable to sleep, Steve worries that they may pierce through the floor.
Keep off the bottom!
Steve begins using the spearfishing gun to drive fish and sharks away. When he feels the bump of a shark, he shoots into the dark water. This drives sharks away for a while. But they always come back.

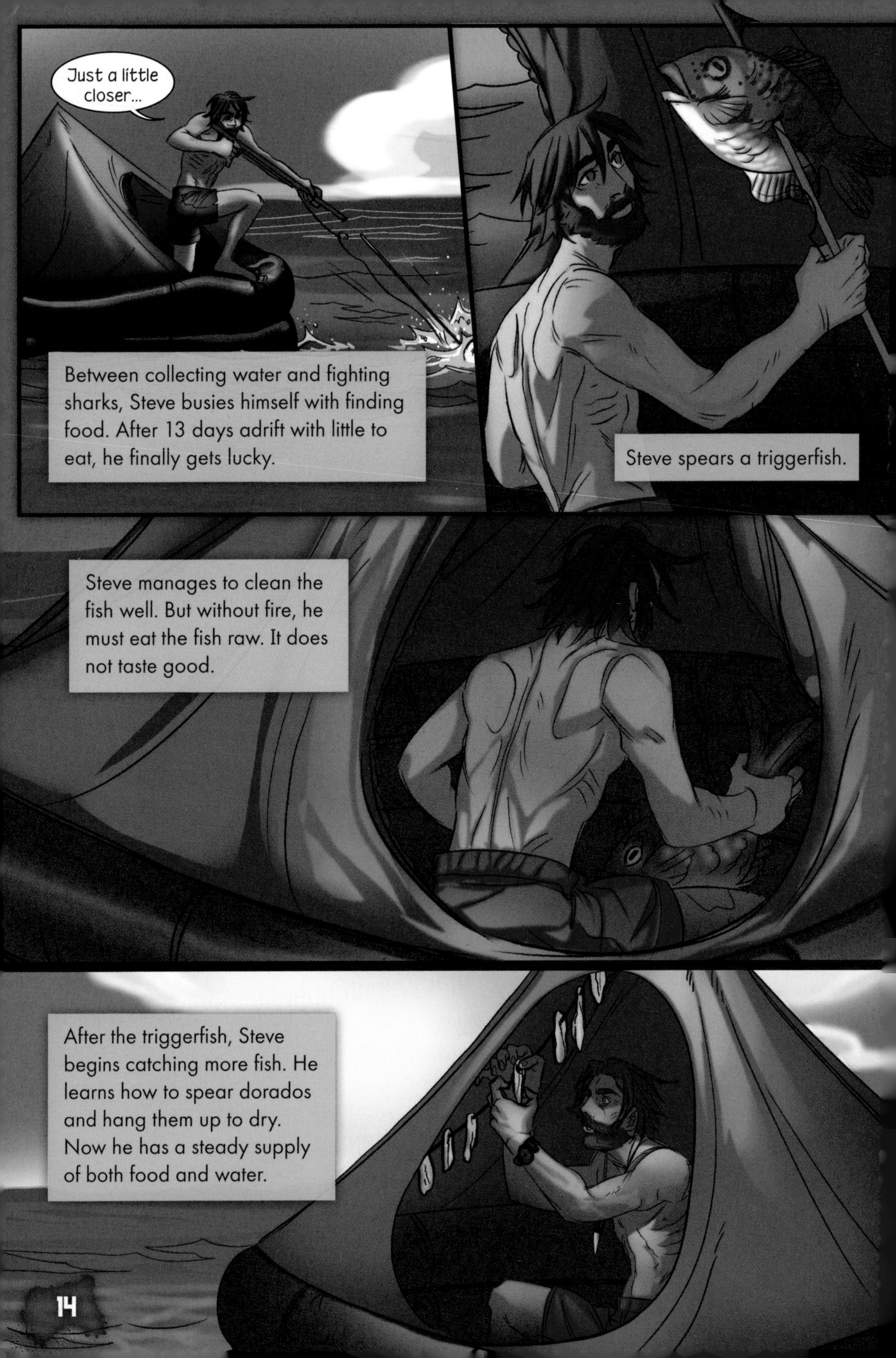
Just a little closer...
Between collecting water and fighting sharks, Steve busies himself with finding food. After 13 days adrift with little to eat, he finally gets lucky.
Steve spears a triggerfish.
Steve manages to clean the fish well. But without fire, he must eat the fish raw. It does not taste good.
After the triggerfish, Steve begins catching more fish. He learns how to spear dorados and hang them up to dry. Now he has a steady supply of both food and water.

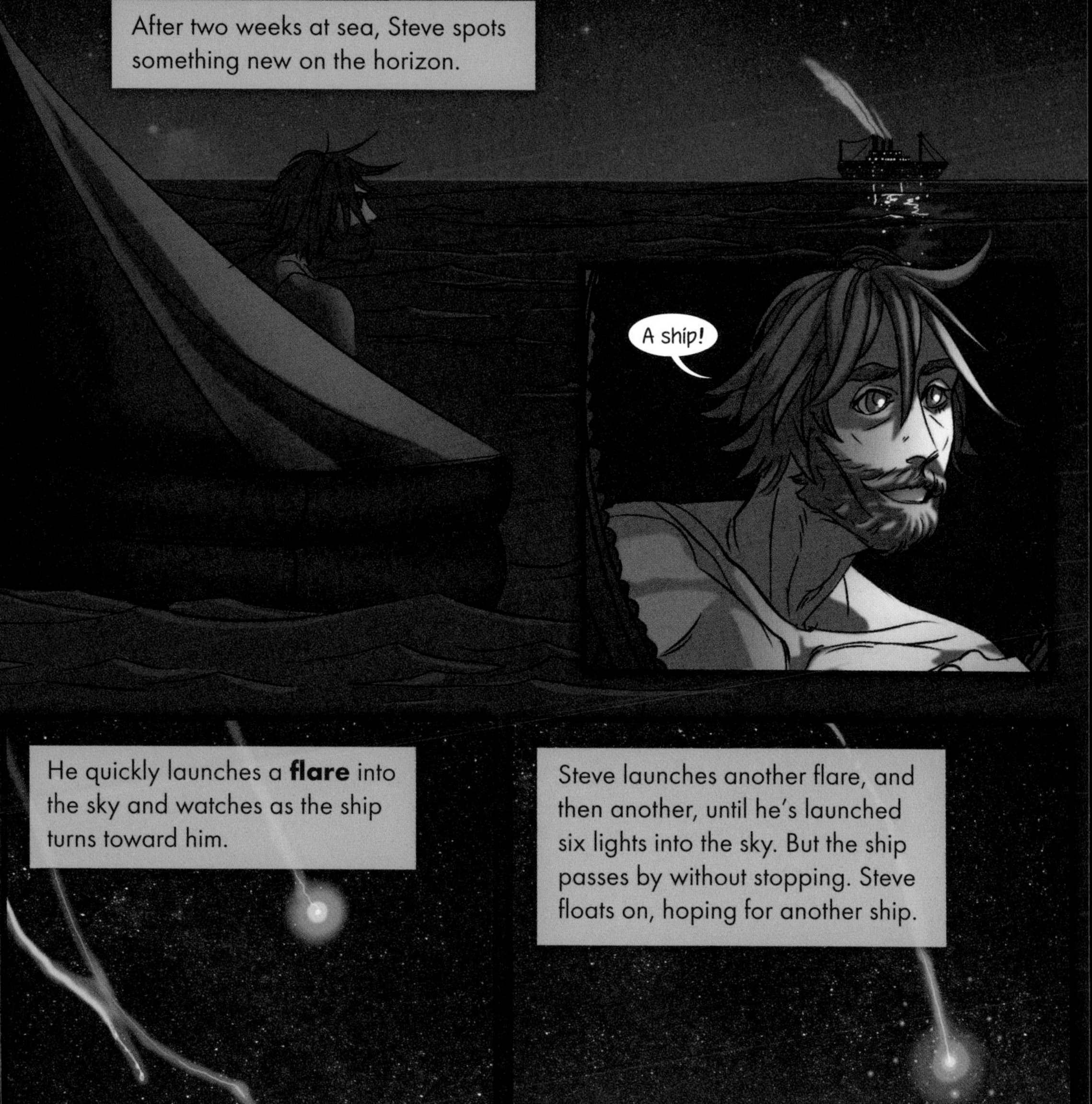
After two weeks at sea, Steve spots something new on the horizon.
A ship!
He quickly launches a **flare** into the sky and watches as the ship turns toward him.
Steve launches another flare, and then another, until he's launched six lights into the sky. But the ship passes by without stopping. Steve floats on, hoping for another ship.

TRIALS AT SEA

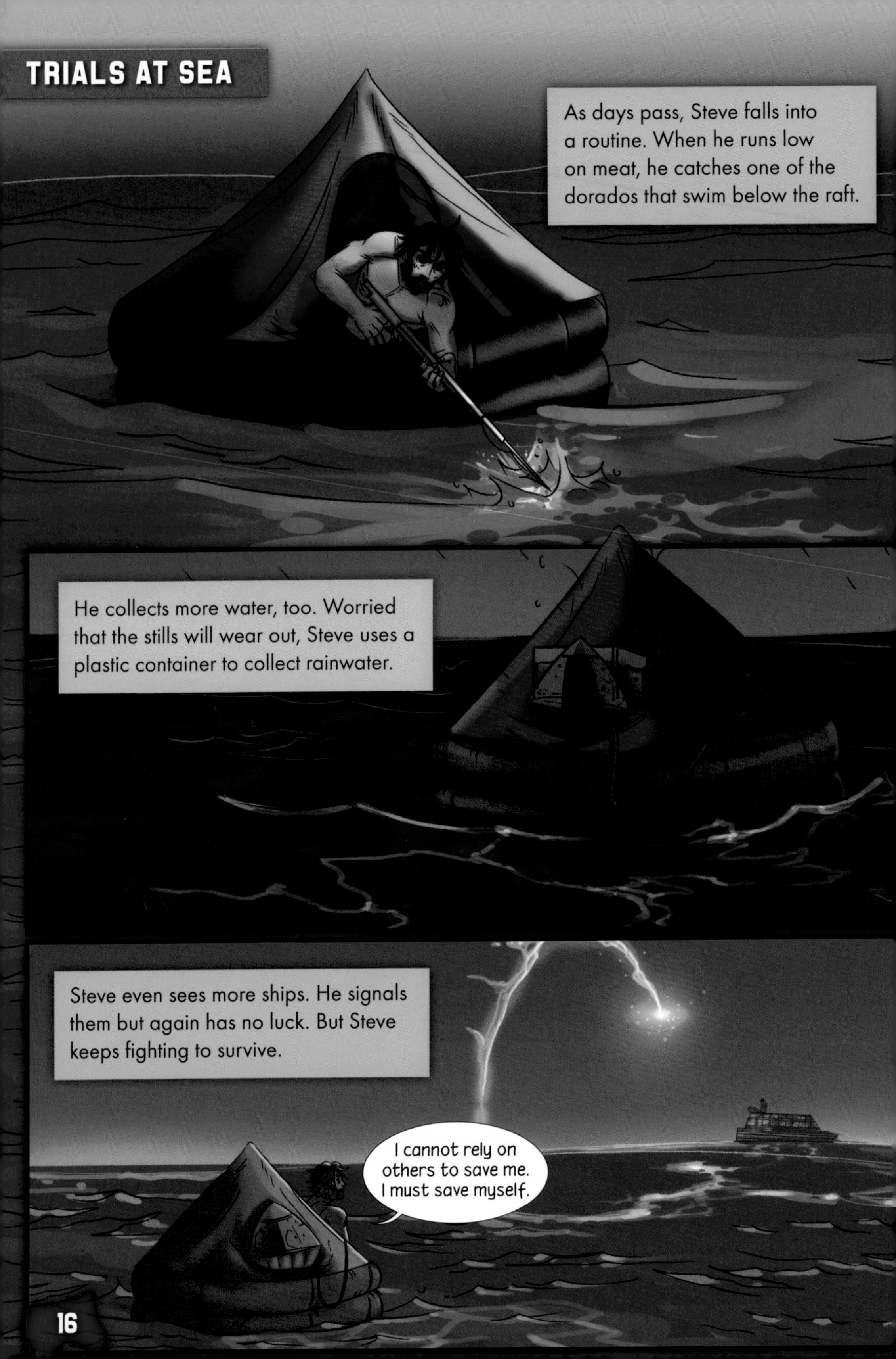
As days pass, Steve falls into a routine. When he runs low on meat, he catches one of the dorados that swim below the raft.
He collects more water, too. Worried that the stills will wear out, Steve uses a plastic container to collect rainwater.
Steve even sees more ships. He signals them but again has no luck. But Steve keeps fighting to survive.
I cannot rely on others to save me. I must save myself.

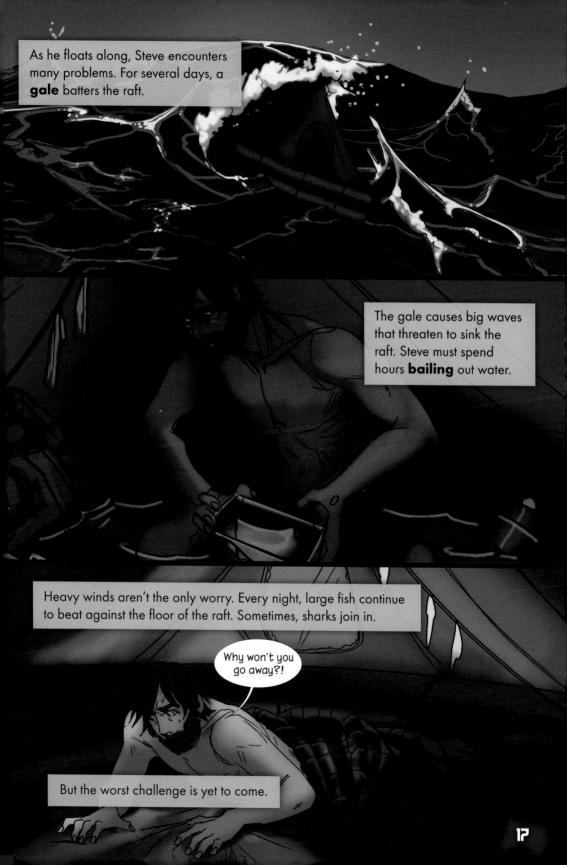

As he floats along, Steve encounters many problems. For several days, a **gale** batters the raft.

The gale causes big waves that threaten to sink the raft. Steve must spend hours **bailing** out water.

Heavy winds aren't the only worry. Every night, large fish continue to beat against the floor of the raft. Sometimes, sharks join in.

Why won't you go away?!

But the worst challenge is yet to come.

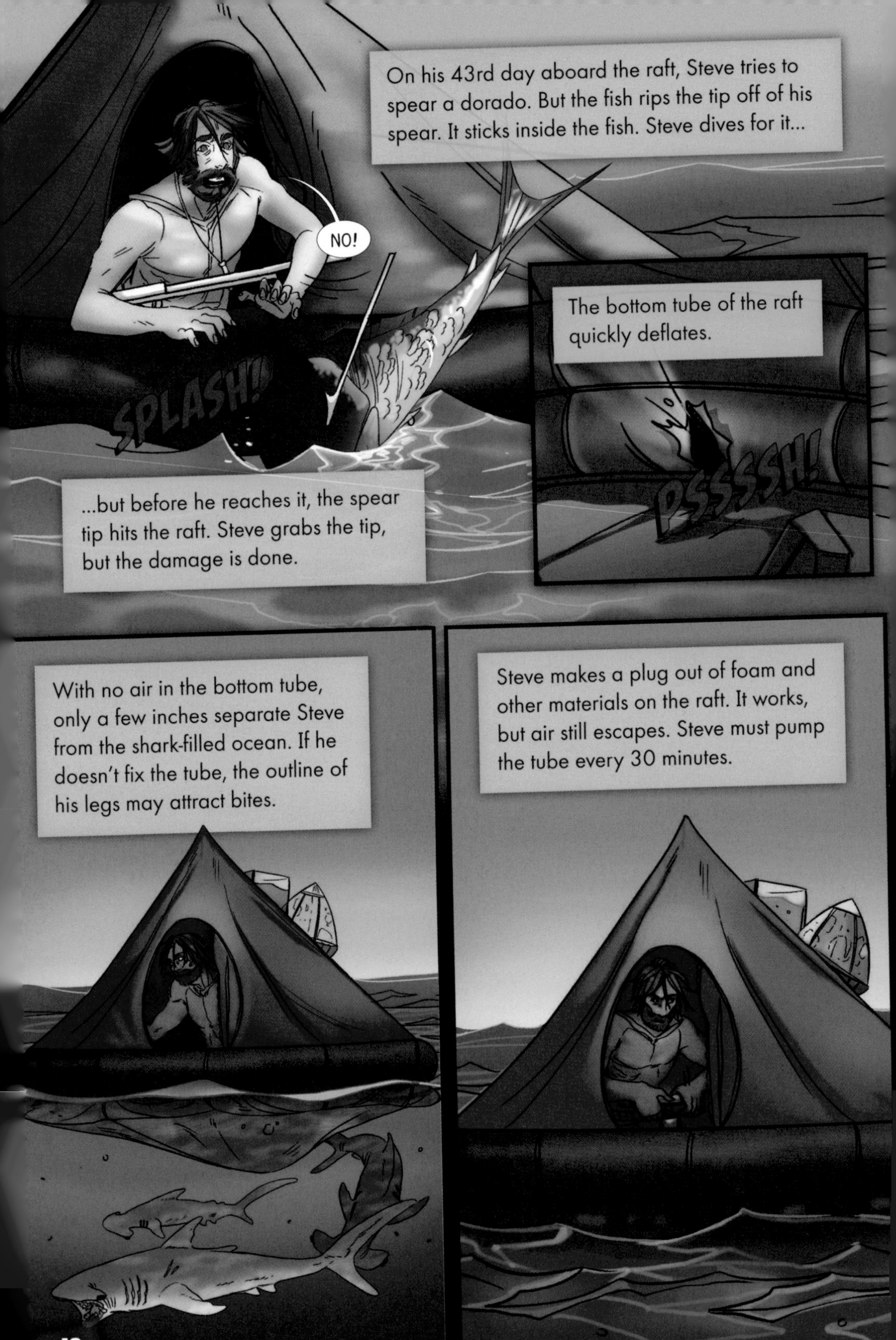
On his 43rd day aboard the raft, Steve tries to spear a dorado. But the fish rips the tip off of his spear. It sticks inside the fish. Steve dives for it...
NO!
SPLASH!
...but before he reaches it, the spear tip hits the raft. Steve grabs the tip, but the damage is done.
The bottom tube of the raft quickly deflates.
PSSSSH!
With no air in the bottom tube, only a few inches separate Steve from the shark-filled ocean. If he doesn't fix the tube, the outline of his legs may attract bites.
Steve makes a plug out of foam and other materials on the raft. It works, but air still escapes. Steve must pump the tube every 30 minutes.

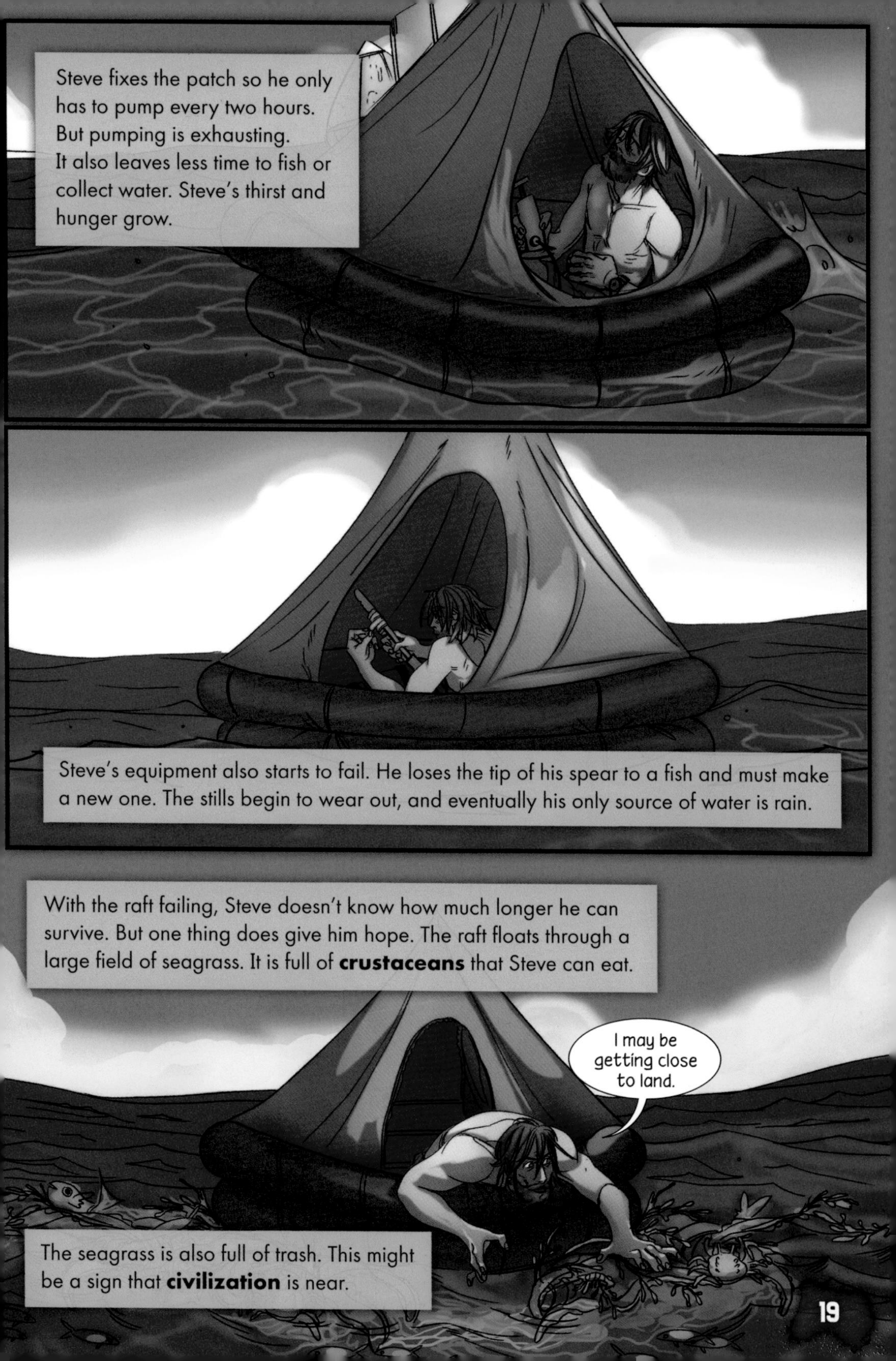
Steve fixes the patch so he only has to pump every two hours. But pumping is exhausting. It also leaves less time to fish or collect water. Steve's thirst and hunger grow.
Steve's equipment also starts to fail. He loses the tip of his spear to a fish and must make a new one. The stills begin to wear out, and eventually his only source of water is rain.
With the raft failing, Steve doesn't know how much longer he can survive. But one thing does give him hope. The raft floats through a large field of seagrass. It is full of **crustaceans** that Steve can eat.
I may be getting close to land.
The seagrass is also full of trash. This might be a sign that **civilization** is near.

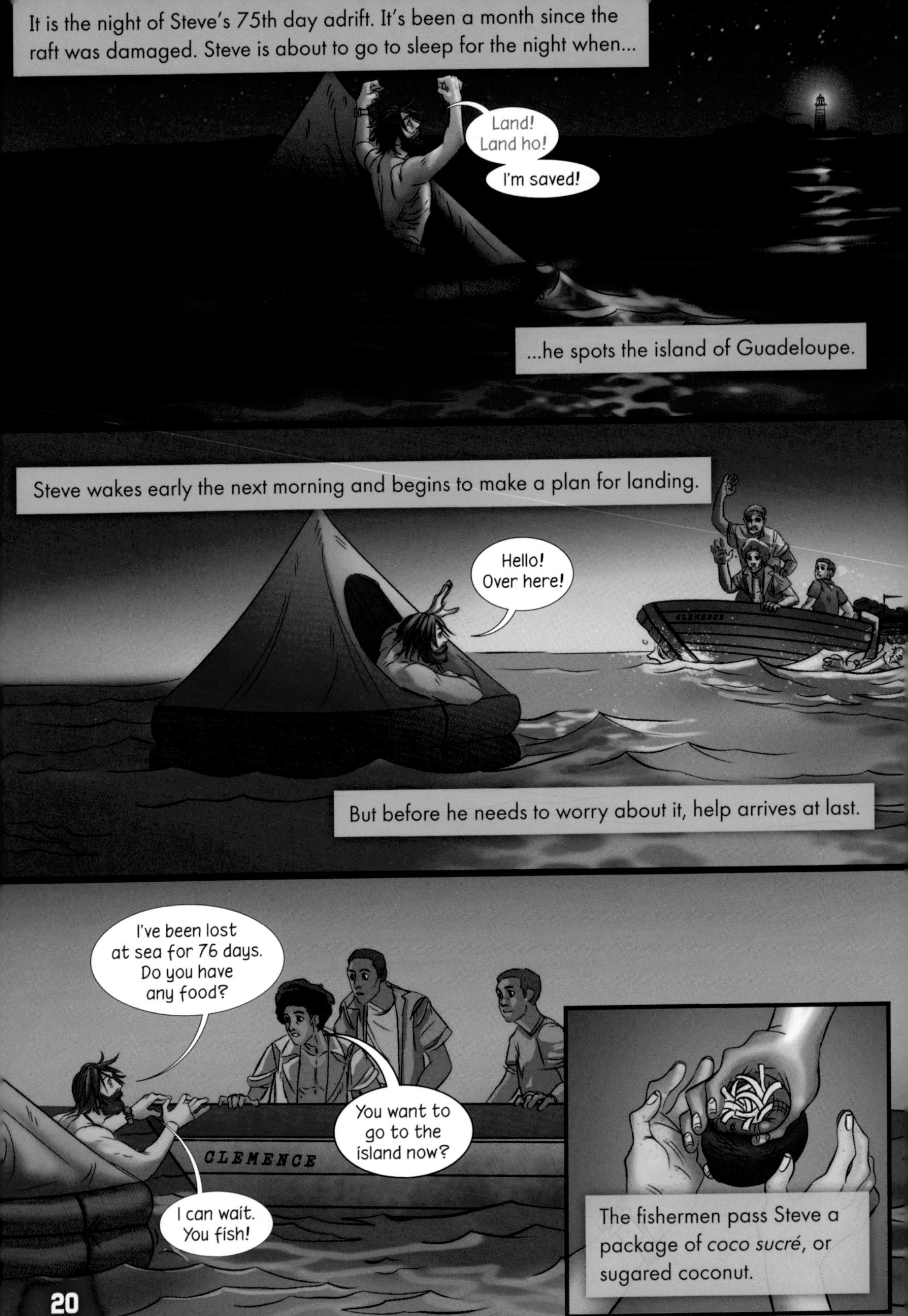
It is the night of Steve's 75th day adrift. It's been a month since the raft was damaged. Steve is about to go to sleep for the night when...
Land! Land ho!
I'm saved!
...he spots the island of Guadeloupe.
Steve wakes early the next morning and begins to make a plan for landing.
Hello! Over here!
But before he needs to worry about it, help arrives at last.
I've been lost at sea for 76 days. Do you have any food?
You want to go to the island now?
I can wait. You fish!
CLEMENCE
The fishermen pass Steve a package of *coco sucré*, or sugared coconut.

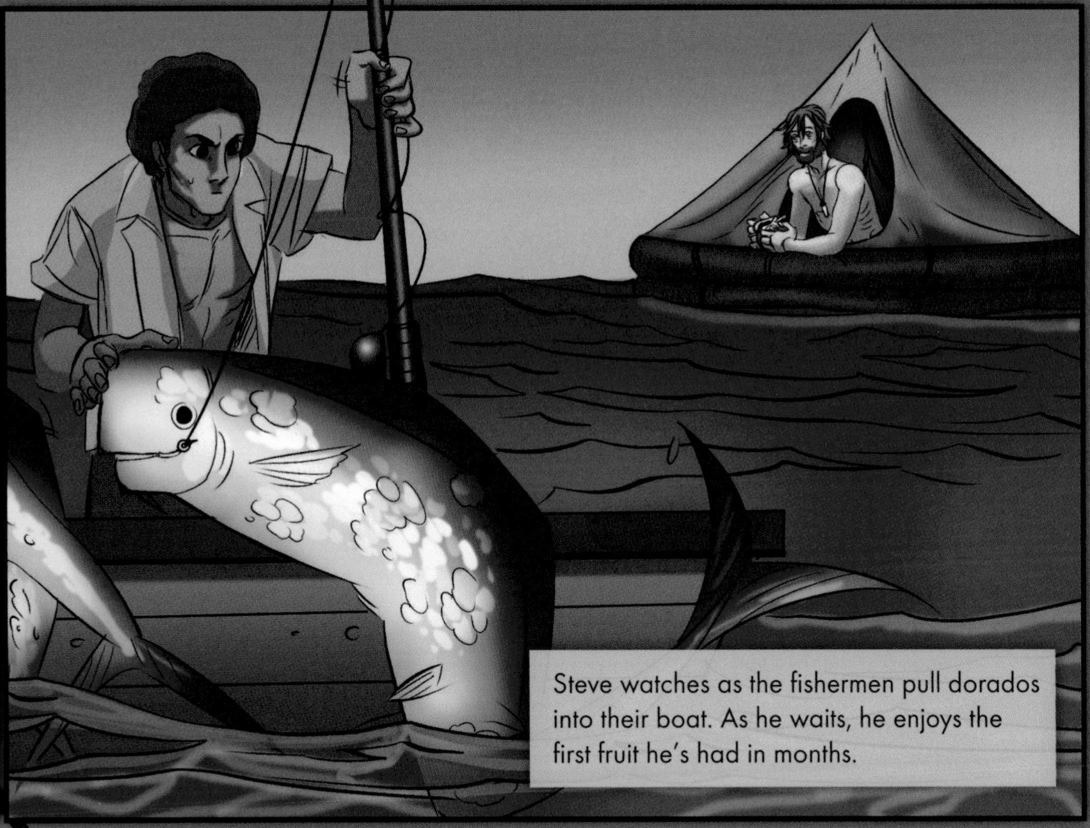
Steve watches as the fishermen pull dorados into their boat. As he waits, he enjoys the first fruit he's had in months.

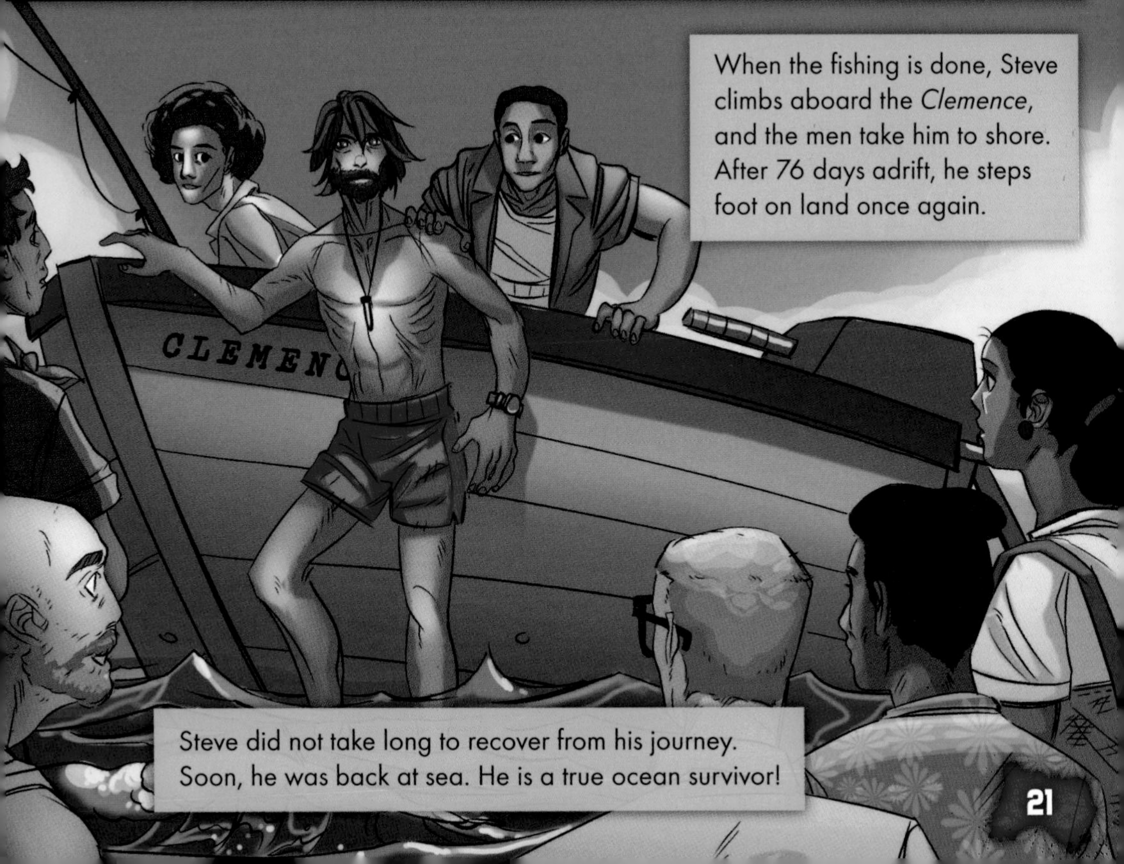
When the fishing is done, Steve climbs aboard the *Clemence*, and the men take him to shore. After 76 days adrift, he steps foot on land once again.
CLEMENC
Steve did not take long to recover from his journey. Soon, he was back at sea. He is a true ocean survivor!

MORE ABOUT STEVE CALLAHAN

- No one knows for sure, but Steve believes the *Napoleon Solo* was sunk by a large whale.
- Steve named his life raft *Rubber Ducky III*.
- After he was rescued by the fishermen, Steve spent only a few hours in the hospital. He spent the next few weeks traveling to nearby islands.
- Steve worked as a consultant for *Life of Pi*, a 2012 movie about a person lost at sea on a small boat. Steve's experience helped the filmmakers make the movie more realistic.

STEVE CALLAHAN TIMELINE

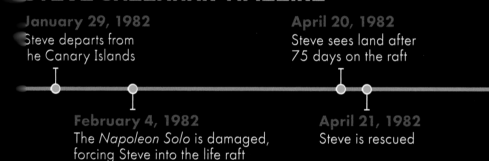

January 29, 1982
Steve departs from the Canary Islands

February 4, 1982
The *Napoleon Solo* is damaged, forcing Steve into the life raft

April 20, 1982
Steve sees land after 75 days on the raft

April 21, 1982
Steve is rescued

STEVE CALLAHAN'S ROUTE

ENGLAND
RHODE ISLAND
BERMUDA
CANARY ISLANDS
GUADELOUPE
BOAT SUNK

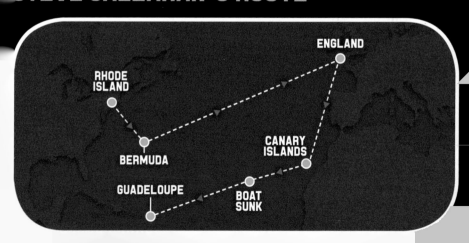

GLOSSARY

architect—a person who designs things to be built

bailing—scooping water out of a boat

capsizing—turning over in water

civilization—a place where people live that has stores, hospitals, and other necessities

crustaceans—animals that have several pairs of legs and hard outer shells; crabs and shrimp are types of crustaceans.

flare—a bright light used to signal to others or attract attention

gale—a strong wind

Mini Transat—a race across the Atlantic Ocean in a certain size of boat

painter—a rope used to tie up or tow a boat

shipping lanes—routes that large boats follow across oceans

sloop—a sailboat with a single mast

solar stills—tools that clean water using the heat of the sun

transatlantic—related to crossing the Atlantic Ocean

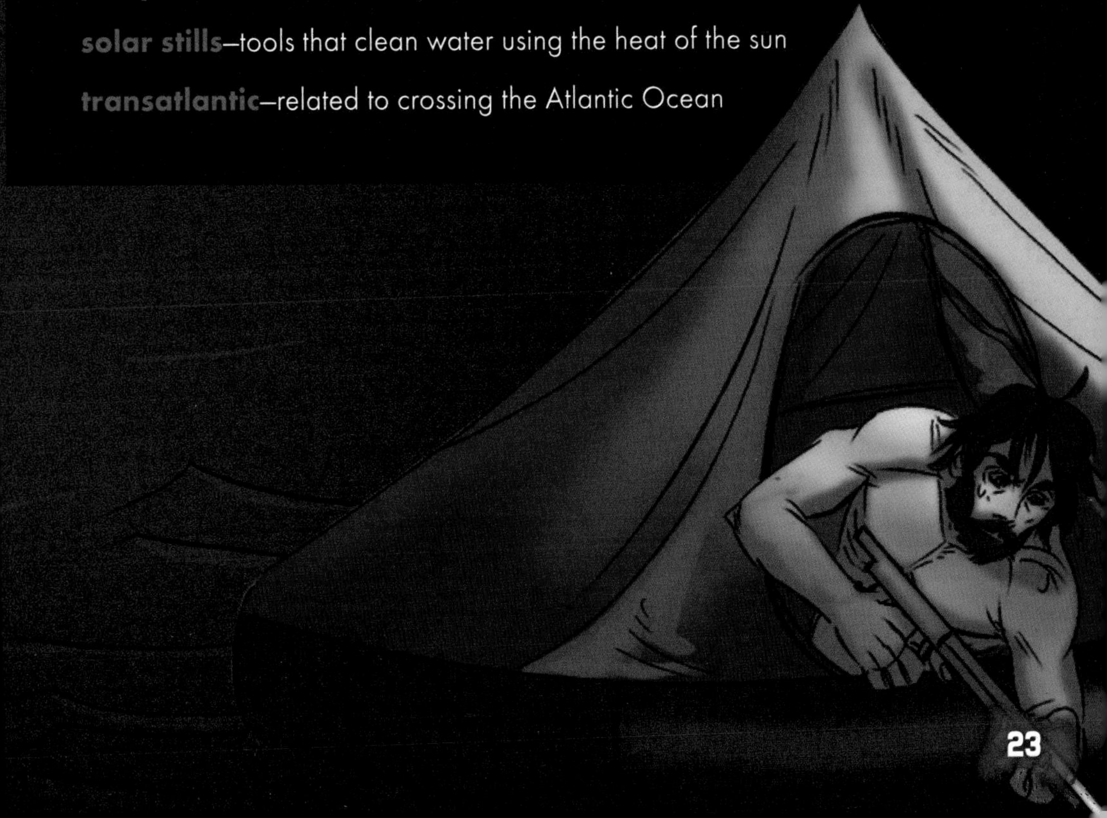

TO LEARN MORE

AT THE LIBRARY

Loh-Hagan, Virginia. *Steven Callahan: Adrift in the Atlantic*. Ann Arbor, Mich.: Cherry Lake Publishing, 2018.

O'Brien, Cynthia. *Ocean Survival Guide*. New York, N.Y.: Crabtree Publishing Company, 2021.

Perish, Patrick. *Survive on a Desert Island*. Minneapolis, Minn.: Bellwether Media, 2017.

ON THE WEB

FACTSURFER

Factsurfer.com gives you a safe, fun way to find more information.

1. Go to www.factsurfer.com
2. Enter "Steve Callahan" into the search box and click 🔍.
3. Select your book cover to see a list of related content.

INDEX